Piano Styles

GW00601958

First Edition. © Barney G Byron. Published by The Wonderful Music Company. 2006. www.wonderfulmusic.co.uk

Order: sales@wonderfulmusic.co.uk Comments: comments@wonderfulmusic.co.uk The Editor: barney@bgbyron.co.uk

Minuet in F

W A Mozart

Allegro♩ = 135

Country Minuet

J Haydn

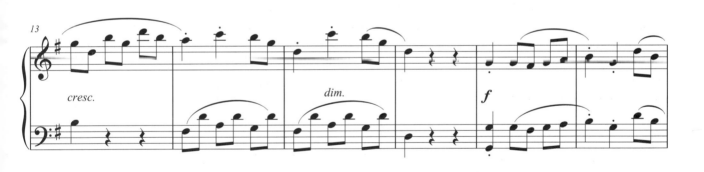

Minuet

The minuet is an elegant court dance that was refined from a peasant dance in 17th century France. The name has now come to mean a piece of music that has all of the characteristics of the minuet dance music despite having no dance attached. Often minuets can be long enough to make up whole movements of symphonies and other multi-movement works.

Minuets have three beats to a bar (very rarely six or even nine) and are of a fairly lively tempo. Historically, minuets were based around two different tunes, one to begin and end the piece (often with a repeat) and one, played by a trio of instruments, to provide a change in the middle. The middle section has retained the name Trio, even when played on a solo piano.

Several famous composers including Mozart and Bach have written Minuets (often called Menuet, Menuett or Minuetto). The later classical composers such as Haydn and Beethoven, composing in the late 18th and early 19th centuries, were instrumental in evolving the minuet into a form of music called a Scherzo. This is a very quick, sometimes humorous version of similar music; these scherzos still generally have the trio section.

Folk Music

Quite simply, folk music is music that has been passed down through generations of people within a community (or music that is composed in traditional style). When the pieces were composed the notes and words would not have been written down. Instead songs were learnt when the musicians and singers joined in with group performances. For this reason, and the fact that much of the music is very old, the composer is hardly ever known and the music is known as Traditional. This way of learning music, or sometimes the music itself, is know as the Oral Tradition.

Each country or region has its own style of folk music that helps to define its national musical identity. It's hard to think of Spanish music without thinking of flamenco guitars; the piece *Leyenda* (meaning legend) is based on this style of traditional music and echoes the rhythms and scales used by the flamenco players.

Sometimes only the melodies and lyrics are known and it is left to the composer or musicians to write the remaining parts (sometimes as they play them). This is true of the book's other example of folk music, *The Curly Headed Ploughboy*. It is an English country-dance tune with a newly written left-hand accompaniment.

The Curly Headed Ploughboy

Folk

Traditional
arr. B Byron

Leyenda*
Folk

Allegro Con moto ♩ = 120

Albeniz

5   Try swapping your hands over so that the RH plays the melody.

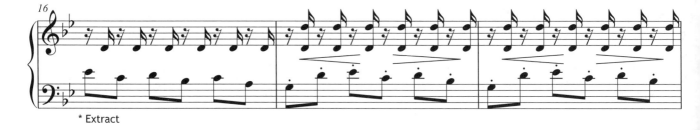

* Extract

molto rall.

Waves

Prelude

B Byron

Prelude

J S Bach

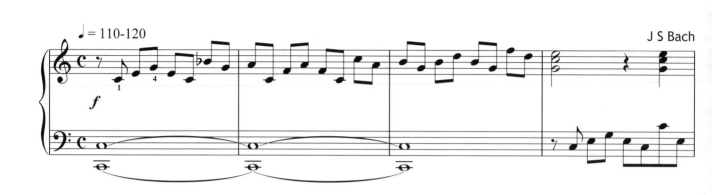

Prelude

In the Renaissance era, the prelude was a piece of music that allowed players to warm their fingers up at the start of a performance and hear how their instruments (often lutes) sounded in the room in which they were performing. The pieces were generally improvised by the performers.

Then in 17th century France, composers began to actually write preludes. They specified only the notes that they wanted performers to play, and left the length of the notes up to the musicians who played the preludes. Later in the 17th century German composers began to write fully prepared preludes to act as introductions and warm-ups for other pieces. In 1722 and 1744 J S Bach wrote two volumes of his famous work *The Well-Tempered Clavier* which features 24 fugues (see page 14) one for each possible major and minor key and each with a prelude. The example in this book is from this well-known and inspiring work.

During the Romantic Period of the 19th century, the prelude became very popular again. Master pianist and composer Chopin is well known for writing preludes that are as beautiful as they are challenging. Frenchman Claude Debussy continued the trend in the later part of the century.

Preludes characteristically contain a repeating pattern - often consisting of broken chords - that varies slightly each time it is played. This is ideal for getting your hands warmed up and getting used to the instrument that you are using, as well as a good way to make interesting pieces of music that are far more than simply warm-up exercises.

Metal (hard rock)

Not so much a piano genre as an often-misunderstood form of music. The common perception is that it is simple, powerful, noisy rock music lacking skill and musicality; this is simply not the case.

There are several changes in tempo and dynamics, many surprisingly beautiful harmonies using 3rds, 6ths, counterpoint and other traditional 'classical' musical techniques. In fact if you took the work of bands such as Iron Maiden or System Of A Down and played them in an orchestra they could easily be mistaken for anything from baroque composer Vivaldi to the more recent Holst and Vaughan Williams.

Often hard rock bands will employ strident, thumping rhythm guitar parts that use chords called *power chords*. These contain the 1st and 5th notes of a musical scale. The key of E minor is popular as it allows low chords and suits the guitar well. Recently there has been a trend to de-tune the guitar to make it lower so that low D chords can be played. Often, straight major or minor scales are replaced by *modes* which have different patterns of tones and semi-tones and can give the music an instantly different atmosphere.

Opus
Metal

B Byron

Fugue

Fugue

A good fugue is one of the most difficult types of piece to compose and play. As well as artistic flair, a good mathematical brain is needed.

For a fugue, you need several 'voices'. These need not be literally human voices but could be any instruments; on a piano or other keyboard instrument it is possible to play more than one voice with each hand. The first voice starts with a theme (tune) and then continues to play other harmonic notes while the second voice comes in with the same starting theme, generally starting on a different key (a style known as imitation). This continues until all the voices are playing together having each played the first tune. Then it is normal to hear the tune in slightly different forms appearing all the way through the piece. The skill comes in making sure that every voice is playing something that sounds good when they are all sounding at the same time.

Fugues tend to sound typically 17th century because this is the time when the likes of J Pachelbel made them popular. Historically J S Bach is the most famous composer of fugues. They are still being written today.

Sonatina

Sonatina

A sonatina is a small sonata. Sonatas have changed drastically over the years and so the rules as to what makes a sonata are quite blurred. Whole books have been written on the subject.

Put simply, a sonata starts with a main theme, this theme gets elaborated and new tunes are introduced before the main tune returns to end the piece. The three sections found in pieces written using *Sonata Form* (more accurately known as *The Sonata Principal*) are:
Exposition: The main tune is shown to us in the tonic key of the piece. More tunes are included later in the section.
Development: The themes get developed and changed, the piece changes key.
Recapitulation: The main tune returns, very often in a different key.

Confusingly, sonatas can have more than one movement and it is very often just the first movement that demonstrates this sonata principal. Sonatinas, being mini-sonatas do generally use this structure.

Sonatina Number 3 in F

Vodyanoi

Polka

B Byron

© 2006 WMC

St Paul's Polka

Trad. arr. B Byron

Polka

The Polka is a type of dance that originated around 1830 from the peasant community in Bohemia, a region that incorporates the central and western parts of the Czech Republic. It soon became popular with people of all classes in several countries. Because of the name many people assume that the Polka is a Polish dance; in fact, the name comes from the Czech word pulka, meaning half. There are two beats to a bar instead of the more commonly seen four, hence each bar is half the size.

After 1835 the polka spread as far north as Norway and became popular in Canada and the USA as well as in central Europe. There is a particularly strong tradition of polka in Irish music and it is even found in some punk songs. The polka sounds different in each country in which it has become popular, evolving in different ways under differing influences. It ranges from quick dance tunes to music resembling the stereotypical German Um-Pa tuba-driven band music.
The two pieces in this book are two contrasting styles of Polka. One is a traditional Norwegian polka, St Paul's Polka and the other is a new piece written in the Russian style.

Etude

An Etude is a piece of music that is designed as an exercise for the fingers to help in a certain area of performance. For example an Etude may concentrate on the playing of different rhythms with each hand at the same time or the playing of scales very quickly. The piece in this book, *Eol's Harp*, concentrates on playing very fast arpeggios that pass between the hands in a tricky time signature. It is a technically difficult piece but most players should be able to enjoy it by choosing small sections to play repeatedly and getting faster and faster with each practice.

Some etudes, notably, those many pieces written by Czerny, are considered to be lacking in melody whereas some, notably those written by Chopin, are works that should be played just as much for their beauty as their technical challenge. Several well known composers such as Debussy, Liszt and Gershwin have all written contrasting etudes.

Eol's Harp
Etude

S. Maikapar

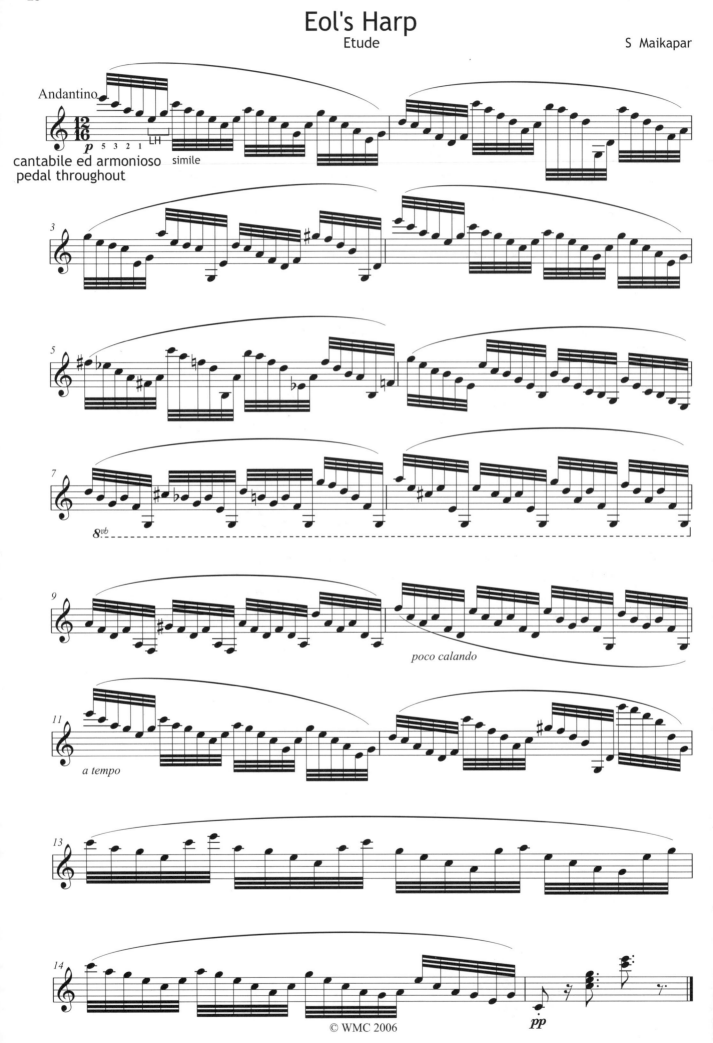

Losing Streak

12 Bar Blues

Try many different speeds
until you find your favourite.
Swing-time.

B G Byron

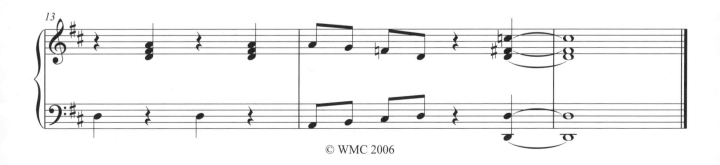

Moonshine
Blues

B Byron

Players with small hands may prefer to play just the bottom note of the right hand melody.
Your own fingering scheme will depend on the size of your hands.

Nocturne

The genre of the Nocturne was first popular in the 19th century. Nocturnes are dreamy, mellow and tranquil pieces that either evoke feelings of the night or are inspired by the night time. Most nocturnes have a gentle left hand part (using arpeggios) and a delicate, sometimes melancholy right hand melody. But like so many types of music there are no written rules for what a nocturne should be.

The Irish composer John Field introduced the name in 1812 and Chopin adopted it and produced several Nocturnes. Chopin's *E flat Nocturne* is included in this book. There were pieces called Nocturnes (or Notturno) before Field but these were really just serenades to be played at night.

There are several pieces from the Romantic period that would have qualified for the name but their composers chose not to refer to them as nocturnes. Beethoven's famous Moonlight Sonata was not considered a nocturne by the great composer himself.

Blues

The history of the blues is a long and complex one, worthy of a whole book to itself. It originated in the USA when slaves and plantation workers adapted the chords of gospel hymns to produce this mournful and expressive form of music. Blues piano quickly became an art form.

Many of the people who developed the blues could not read or write words or music and so the pieces were often improvised; this meant that standard chord structures were necessary so that musicians knew what they were doing. The most commonly used structure is called *12 Bar Blues*. To work out the chords needed for 12 Bar Blues you have to know what the 1st, 4th and 5th notes of the piece's key scale are. 12 bar blues in D uses the D, G & A chords because D, G & A are the 1st, 4th and 5th notes. Each bar is based around one of these three chords. The piece *Losing Streak* is a 12 Bar Blues in D major. Look at each bar and try to work out the chord structure; this will aid your understanding of the pattern. The first left hand note in each section will be a big help.
Most blues music uses one of the three scales that are known as the Blues Scales and are, simply, a combination of some notes from both the major and minor scales. They use the note between the 4th and 5th elements of a scale, an unusual note that is found in neither the major nor minor scales.

Alone
Nocturne

B G Byron

Andante Cantabile

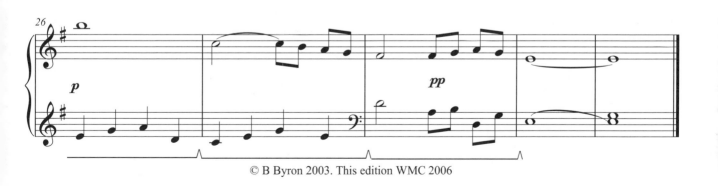

Nocturne in E♭

F Chopin